THE YOUNG PERSON'S GUIDE TO THE

# OPERA

THE YOUNG PERSON'S GUIDE TO THE

# OPERA

IN ASSOCIATION WITH

## THE ROYAL OPERA HOUSE

WITH MUSIC FROM THE GREAT OPERAS ON CD

BOOK WRITTEN BY

### ANITA GANERI AND NICOLA BARBER

PAVILION

First published in Great Britain in 2001 by
PAVILION BOOKS LTD
London House, Great Eastern Wharf
Parkgate Road, London SW11 4NQ

Copyright © Pavilion Books 2001
Text copyright © Anita Ganeri 2001 and Nicola Barber 2001
*About the CD* text, pages 50–51 © Warwick Thompson 2001
For copyright of photographs, see p.55

Consultants: Paul Reeve and Francesca Franchi, Royal Opera House, Covent Garden, London
Additional Information: Ian Campbell, San Diego Opera
Designer: Nigel Partridge
Editor: Jo Fletcher-Watson
Picture Researcher: Felicity Harvey

A CIP catalogue record for this book is available
from the British Library

ISBN 1 86205 3863

Set in ITC Garamond
Printed in China by Imago

2  4  6  8  10  9  7  5  3  1

This book can be ordered direct from the publisher.
Please contact the Marketing Department.
But try your bookshop first.

*Frontispiece: Rosina Daintymouth makes her entrance from the gingerbread house in San Diego Opera's 1999 production of* Hansel and Gretel *composed by Engelbert Humperdinck. The designs are by children's illustrator Maurice Sendak*
*Front cover: Diana Soviero as Cio-Cio-San in Madama Butterfly, Royal Opera House, 1993*

# Contents

# Introduction

A warm welcome to the world of opera! Since opera began some 400 years ago, it has thrilled audiences with its stirring singing, its larger-than-life characters, and its dazzling blend of spectacle, passion, and action. A visit to the opera is an experience you will not forget. Today, though, opera is not only to be heard in the magnificence of an opera house. It accompanies films, advertisements, and even European football matches – you've probably heard some of the great works of opera without even realizing.

This book looks at opera from its earliest days, in the courts of Italy and France, to opera at its most modern. Read the stories behind some of the greatest operas, and meet some of the most famous – and infamous – opera singers of all. Follow professional singers as they prepare for the roles of their lives. Take a look backstage at some of the greatest opera houses, and see the work of the musicians, set designers, and costume designers who help to bring an opera to the stage. The accompanying CD (see pages 50–51) includes extracts from some of the world's best-loved operas, which you can enjoy while reading *The Young Person's Guide to the Opera* – the perfect introduction to opera at its best.

*(left) The Royal Opera House's 1995 production of* Götterdämmerung

# What Is Opera?

Welcome to the opera! As the curtain rises, the audience is transported to another world – one of action, passion, and spectacle. Stirring music, stunning scenery, and exciting plots all make a visit to the opera an experience to remember.

## What is opera?

T he word *opera* comes from the Italian *opera in musica,* which means "works or plays in music." An opera is a play in which the characters sing their lines rather than speak them. It is a mixture of many different types of art and entertainment, combining music, drama, dance, and often elaborate costumes and scenery. To become a great opera singer, you must understand all aspects of this complicated and exciting art form.

*(right) A scene from* Carmen *showing Lillas Pastia's Tavern*

ABOUT THE CD

The CD that accompanies this book features extracts from some of the most popular operas. You can find out more about them throughout the book. The composers and the dates of the first performances are given here.

*Die Zauberflöte*
(*The Magic Flute*)
Wolfgang Amadeus Mozart, 1791

*Il barbiere di Siviglia*
(*The Barber of Seville*)
Gioacchino Rossini, 1816

*L'elisir d'amore*
(*The Elixir of Love*)
Gaetano Donizetti, 1832

*Rigoletto*
Giuseppe Verdi, 1851

*Il trovatore*
(*The Troubadour*)
Giuseppe Verdi, 1851

*Die Walküre* (*The Valkyrie*)
Richard Wagner, 1870

*Die Fledermaus* (*The Bat*)
Johann Strauss, 1874

*Carmen*
Georges Bizet, 1875

*Tosca*
Giacomo Puccini, 1900

*Madama Butterfly*
Giacomo Puccini, 1904

*(left) Opera is not just about singing – it combines music, dance, elaborate costumes, and action, in an unforgettable blend of entertainment*

## Words and music

In an opera, words and music are used together to tell a story. The words of an opera are called the *libretto*, an Italian word meaning "little book" (see page 34 for more details). The music, or score, is made up of both singing and instrumental music. The task of the opera singers, conductor, and orchestra is to take the libretto and score and transform them into a great performance.

## Putting on an opera

Putting on an opera is a huge – and costly – task. Apart from the singers, a great many people spend months working hard behind the scenes. Companies have to choose each season's operas carefully, balancing old and new, tragic and comic, to keep audiences entertained.

# How Opera Began

The first operas were performed in Italy about 400 years ago. They were musical dramas performed at court for the royal families and their guests, usually composed to celebrate special occasions such as royal weddings.

## LA DAFNE

The story of Dafne comes from *Metamorphoses* by the Roman poet Ovid. The god Apollo falls in love with Dafne, a beautiful nymph. To escape from Apollo, Dafne asks the gods to turn her into a laurel tree. From that time on, the laurel tree is sacred to Apollo.

## Musical dramas

The earliest operas grew out of musical dramas based on Greek or Roman myths. These were composed by a group of noblemen, poets, and musicians who lived in Florence, Italy, in the 1570s and 1580s. They were called the Florentine Camerata. One member of the Camerata, Jacopo Peri (1561–1633), composed the first known opera, *La Dafne*, in 1597. The libretto was written by the poet Ottavio Rinuccini (1562–1621). Peri himself took the part of Apollo, and the opera was a great success. Sadly, most of the music for the opera has been lost, so we do not know what it sounded like.

*(right) An outdoor performance of an Italian musical drama*

## Wedding music

In 1600 Peri and Rinuccini created the opera *Euridice*, based on a popular Greek legend. The hero Orpheus visits the underworld to beg Pluto, god of the dead, to free his beloved wife, Euridice, who has died from a snakebite. Orpheus plays his lyre for Pluto so beautifully that Pluto agrees to grant Orpheus's wish. In the original legend, Orpheus must lead Euridice out of the underworld without looking back at her. But Orpheus cannot help himself. He looks back and loses Euridice forever. Peri composed the opera for the wedding of King Henry IV of France and Maria de Medici in Florence, so he gave the story a happy ending to mark the joyful occasion.

*(right) A painting showing Orpheus rescuing Euridice from the underworld*

# Opera Moves On

In the 1600s, opera spread from Florence to other Italian cities such as Venice and Rome. Arias gradually became an important part of opera, allowing the characters to express their thoughts and feelings, and the singers to show off their vocal skills. Toward the end of the 1600s, opera began its spread to other countries in Europe.

## Music by Monteverdi

The greatest composer of early operas was the Italian Claudio Monteverdi (1567–1643). The composer at the court of the Duke of Mantua, he was commissioned to write an opera based on the Orpheus myth (see page 11). His great opera *L'Orfeo* was first performed in 1607. This was the first time in opera that instruments were given an important role. Monteverdi's last opera, *L'incoronazione di Poppea* (*The Coronation of Poppaea*), was performed in Venice in 1642. The opera tells the story of the Roman emperor Nero and his mistress Poppaea. It was the first opera known to be based on historical fact rather than on legend.

### STAR SINGERS

The Italian contralto Adriana Basile (1580–1640) was the most famous opera singer of her day. Monteverdi thought very highly of her and may have written the part of Orpheus for her. No one knows if she ever sang it.

*(left) Claudio Monteverdi (1567–1643)*

*(above) A performance of an early opera*

## Opera in France

In France a distinct style of opera developed. It was less flamboyant than Italian opera, with simpler songs and more expressive melodies. Italian-born Jean-Baptiste Lully (1632–1687), the court composer, wrote operas and ballets for King Louis XIV. His first opera, *Cadmus and Hermione*, was performed in 1674. It was a great success. King Louis XIV attended the first night and is said to have been "extraordinarily satisfied with this superb spectacle."

## Opera in England

The first English opera was *Dido and Aeneas* by Henry Purcell (1659–1695). Based on Greek myth, it tells the story of the love between Dido, Queen of Carthage, and Aeneas, the hero of the Trojan Wars. Purcell was asked to write the opera for a London girls' school, and the pupils put on the first performance in 1689. Because of this, the opera was only an hour long and the parts were not too difficult to sing.

*(left) A scene from Purcell's* King Arthur, *written in 1691*

# Opera for Everyone

By the late seventeenth century, opera had become hugely popular. Dukes and noblemen set up opera companies and sponsored grand productions to show off their wealth. Ordinary people enjoyed opera, too. At least sixteen public opera houses had been built in Venice alone, and hundreds of operas were produced.

## DA CAPO SINGING

The da capo aria became a key feature of opera at this time. *Da capo* is Italian for "from the head" (that is, from the beginning). A da capo aria has three parts, where the third part repeats the first. In the third part, singers are expected to add their own trills and difficult notes to make the singing more spectacular.

## Serious opera

In the late 1600s and early 1700s, Italian opera was all the rage, and many non-Italian composers wrote operas in the Italian style and language. The leading types of Italian opera were *opera seria* (serious opera) and *opera buffa* (comic opera). Opera seria were often based on stories from ancient Greek and Roman mythology. They were known for their spectacular stage effects, such as storms or earthquakes, and for the brilliant singing required from performers.

## Comic opera

Opera buffa began as short musical sketches performed between the acts of opera seria. Later they became operas in their own right. Unlike opera seria, they dealt with characters from everyday life who found themselves in comical situations. *La serva padrona* (*The Maid Mistress*) by Giovanni Pergolesi (1710–1736) was one of the first opera buffa. First performed in 1733, it tells the story of how the maid Serpina tricks her master, Uberto, into marrying her so that she becomes mistress of the house.

(below) Giovanni Pergolesi (1710–1736)

*(right) An etching from around 1728 showing a performance of Handel's* Flavio. *The female singer is the Italian soprano Francesca Cuzzoni.*

## Handel in England

I
n 1710 the German composer George Frideric Handel (1685–1759) arrived in England and quickly put opera on the map. His first London opera, *Rinaldo*, was performed in 1711 to great acclaim. For the next thirty years, Handel provided English audiences with his own dazzling style of opera seria, written in Italian.

*(left) A portrait of George Frideric Handel, whose compositions thrilled English audiences in the eighteenth century*

# Classical Opera

In the mid-eighteenth century, audiences began to turn against opera seria, with complicated plots and singing. This led to a new style of opera called classical opera. The classical period lasted from about 1750 to 1820.

## The Beggar's Opera

In 1728 a new opera was heard in London. Called a ballad opera, *The Beggar's Opera* had lyrics by English poet and playwright John Gay (1685–1732). The lyrics were set to music borrowed from existing operas and folk songs. The opera was a huge success. It opened on January 29 and ran for sixty-three nights. The audience loved the cast of thieves and highwaymen, and found the opera easy to understand because it was sung in English.

*(right)* The Beggar's Opera, with lyrics by the poet John Gay, was a popular success

---

**ENCORE! ENCORE!**

Emperor Leopold II of Austria so enjoyed a performance of *Il matrimonio segreto* (*The Secret Marriage*) by Domenico Cimarosa in 1792 that he invited the cast to supper and then had them perform the whole opera all over again.

---

**DID YOU KNOW?**

In 1928 German poet Bertholt Brecht and composer Kurt Weill wrote *Die Dreigroschenoper* (*The Threepenny Opera*), based on *The Beggar's Opera*. The music was a mixture of jazz, cabaret, and folk music, and was performed by a jazz orchestra.

John Gay's *The Beggar's Opera* was so successful that John Rich, manager of the opera house where it was performed, decided to build a new opera house in London's Covent Garden. This is where the Royal Opera House now stands.

*(above) An engraved portrait of Christoph Willibald Gluck*

## Reforming the opera

**G**erman composer Christoph Willibald Gluck (1714–1787) helped change the course of opera. Instead of using far-fetched plots and unbelievable characters, he tried to simplify the action and make the characters more natural. He used the music to move the story along rather than as a showcase for the singers. The first opera Gluck wrote in the new style was *Orféo ed Euridice* (*Orpheus and Euridice*) in 1762.

## Magical Mozart

**T**he greatest classical composer of all was Wolfgang Amadeus Mozart (1756–1791). Mozart wrote his first opera in 1768 when he was just twelve years old. With the librettist Lorenzo Da Ponte (1749–1838), Mozart created three of his best-loved operas – *Le nozze di Figaro* (*The Marriage of Figaro*, 1786), *Don Giovanni* (1787), and *Così fan tutte* (*All Women Do So*, 1790). Mozart's operas have brilliant music, witty characters, and stirring themes of love, loyalty, and revenge. They are still as popular with audiences today as when they were first performed.

*(right) A portrait of Wolfgang Amadeus Mozart (1756–1791)*

### FIGARO, FIGARO

*Le nozze di Figaro* (*The Marriage of Figaro*) is based on the second of three plays by French playwright Pierre de Beaumarchais. The story was well-known in Mozart's time. It tells of preparations for the wedding of Figaro, barber to Count Almaviva, and Susanna, the Countess's maid. Rossini based his 1816 opera *Il barbiere di Siviglia* (*The Barber of Seville*) on Beaumarchais' first play.

# Grand Opera

By the mid-1800s, opera was at its height. Composers could no longer rely on royal patronage; they were under pressure to produce box-office hits. With its stirring music, spectacular stage sets, and exciting crowd scenes, grand opera became very popular with aristocrats and ordinary people.

## Romantic opera

Romantic operas tell stories of nature, folklore, and the supernatural, and emphasize feelings and emotions. One of the greatest Romantic operas is *Der Freischütz* (*The Freeshooter*) by German composer Carl Maria von Weber (1786–1826). Set in a forest, the opera tells of the struggle between good and evil. Powerful music sets the scene and portrays the forces of nature.

## Beautiful singing

*(right) The Italian composer Gioacchino Rossini*

The great nineteenth-century composers Gioacchino Rossini (1792–1868), Gaetano Donizetti (1797–1848), and Vincenzo Bellini (1801–1835) wrote brilliant operas in the bel canto style. *Bel canto* means "beautiful singing" in Italian. These operas stress beautiful singing techniques, tone, and phrasing. Bellini's *Norma* contains good examples of the bel canto style.

### DID YOU KNOW?

The great German composer Ludwig van Beethoven (1770–1827) wrote only one opera, *Fidelio* (1805). Its first performance was a disaster. The singers complained about the music, and the audience found it difficult to understand. Beethoven revised the opera in 1806 and again in 1814. The third version proved much more popular and is the one performed today.

When Queen Victoria went to see *Fidelio* in 1851, she was so disgusted by the sloppy appearance of the actors playing soldiers that she insisted real guardsmen be used instead. Soldiers from the Household Regiments were used in all operas from then on. The last opera they appeared in was *Il trovatore* in 1978.

*(below) Piero Faggioni rehearsing Plácido Domingo in a 1989 production of* Il trovatore

*(left) Act I, scene ii, of* Aïda

## Verdi and grand opera

Italian composer Giuseppe Verdi (1813–1901) wrote some of the grandest operas of all. His masterpieces include *Rigoletto* (1851), *Il trovatore* (*The Troubadour*, 1853), and *La traviata* (*The Wayward One*, 1853). Verdi became so famous that the khedive (ruler) of Egypt asked him to write a new opera for the opening of the Cairo Opera House. The result was *Aïda* (1871). Set in ancient Egypt, *Aïda* tells the story of the doomed love affair between Aïda, an Ethiopian slave, and Radamès, an Egyptian soldier. It was grand opera at its grandest. The production even included a ballet with camels and elephants onstage.

## Richard Wagner

One of the greatest composers of the nineteenth century was the German Richard Wagner (1813–1883). He called his operas "music-dramas" and believed that all parts of the production – the music, singing, acting, and staging – were equally important. By linking them, he created a great theatrical experience for the audience. Unusually, Wagner wrote the music and libretto himself, creating some of the most powerful operas ever heard.

## The Ring of the Nibelung

Wagner based his epic opera cycle, *Der Ring des Nibelungen* (*The Ring of the Nibelung*), on ancient Norse and German legends. Three water nymphs, the Rhinemaidens, guard a hoard of gold on the bottom of the River Rhine. Alberich, a Nibelung dwarf, steals the gold and makes a ring from it. Whoever wears the ring has magical powers and will rule the world. The ring changes hands many times, until finally it causes the downfall of gods, whose greed for power destroys them.

*(above) Richard Wagner (1813–1883)*

*(left) An illustration of Brünnhilde from* The Ring of the Nibelung *by Richard Wagner*

### DID YOU KNOW?

Performed as a whole, without intervals, *The Ring of the Nibelung* would last for more than fifteen hours. For this reason, each opera in the *Ring* is usually performed on a different day. The last *Ring* cycle performed by the Royal Opera House was in September–October 1998. If the lengths of all the performances were added together, this cycle would have lasted fifteen hours and seventeen minutes – that's nineteen hours and twelve minutes with the intervals!

*(above)* Die Walküre *1989*

## Musical themes

Wagner used short pieces of music to introduce listeners to ideas, characters, or specific parts of the action. These pieces are repeated as reminders throughout the opera. They are called *leitmotifs*, a German word meaning "leading themes." In *The Ring of the Nibelung*, for example, leitmotifs are used to identify the Valkyries, the giants, the ring, and feelings such as greed and hate. Every time one of these elements appears, its particular leitmotif is played.

## Four operas

The *Ring of the Nibelung* is actually made up of four operas: *Das Rheingold* (*The Rhinegold*, 1869), *Die Walküre* (*The Valkyrie*, 1870), *Siegfried* (1876), and *Götterdämmerung* (*The Twilight of the Gods*, 1876). The whole cycle was first performed at the opening of the Festspielhaus in Bayreuth, Germany, in 1876. This opera house was specially built for Wagner's work (see page 42).

*(left) A 1996 Royal Opera production of* Siegfried

21

# Twentieth-Century Opera

During the late nineteenth century, composers in countries such as Russia, Czechoslovakia, and France developed their own styles of opera, often using traditional stories and melodies from their native countries. These operas became known as nationalist operas.

## Czech opera

The first nationalist opera composer in Czechoslovakia was Bedřich Smetana (1824–1884). His best-known opera, *The Bartered Bride*, set in a village in Bohemia, tells the light-hearted story of two lovers, Mařenka and Jeník. Smetana uses melodies and rhythms from Czech folk songs throughout the opera.

### THE "MIGHTY FIVE"

Glinka's use of his country's musical traditions started a trend in Russia. His most famous followers were a group of five nationalist composers known as the "Mighty Five" or "Mighty Fistful." The best-known of the Mighty Five were Modest Mussorgsky (1839–1881) and Nicolay Rimsky-Korsakov (1844–1908). After Mussorgsky's death, Rimsky-Korsakov decided to "improve" Mussorgsky's most successful opera, *Boris Godunov*, by rewriting some of the music. Today the opera is usually heard in Mussorgsky's original version.

*(left) Act III of a Royal Opera production of* The Bartered Bride *in 1998*

By the time he wrote *Madama Butterfly*, Puccini was already famous and he probably expected his latest opera to be a roaring success. But the first night was a disaster. Several of Puccini's rivals had hired hecklers to sit in the audience and disrupt the performance. There was so much hissing and shouting of rude comments that the performance was nearly abandoned. Not to be defeated, Puccini reworked parts of the opera, and the next performance was a triumph.

*(below) Giacomo Puccini (1858–1924)*

## The "Father of Russian Music"

The founder of the nationalist movement in Russia was Mikhail Glinka (1804–1857). His opera *A Life for the Tsar* takes its story from an episode in Russian history, when a Russian peasant sacrificed his own life to save his emperor (tsar) from a Polish uprising. Glinka used Russian folk tunes and the sounds of folk instruments, such as the balalaika, to create a truly Russian opera.

## Verismo opera

The beginning of the twentieth century saw the rise of gritty, real-life stories as the subject for operas. These were known as *verismo* opera. The term describes perfectly the work of the Italian composer Giacomo Puccini (1858–1924). His famous operas *La bohème* (*The Bohemians*), *Madama Butterfly*, and *Tosca* are still frequently performed in opera houses all over the world. The secret of Puccini's success lies in his powerful, memorable tunes and his emotional stories. Puccini's operas often end in tragedy (in all of the operas named above, the heroine dies in the final scene).

*(left) The young lovers, Rodolfo and Mimì, in Puccini's* La bohème

# Modern Opera

During the twentieth century, composers moved away from romantic styles and grand opera. They experimented with new musical sounds such as jazz songs or cabaret music in their operas, and they used new subjects for their plots such as nonsense stories or real-life events from modern history.

## Richard Strauss

Richard Strauss (1864–1949) conducted his first opera in 1894 and completed his last one, *Capriccio*, in 1941. Many people consider him to be the last of the German Romantic composers because he wrote such beautiful melodies. But Strauss was also an experimenter, writing complicated, chaotic-sounding music in his operas *Salome* and *Elektra*. His most famous opera, *Der Rosenkavalier* (*The Knight of the Rose*), was so successful when it was first performed in 1911 that special "Rosenkavalier" trains brought people from all over Germany to the city of Dresden to see the show.

*(right) The Marschallin and Baron Ochs in* Der Rosenkavalier, *Strauss's most famous opera*

### THE NOSE

One of the most bizarre plots used by a twentieth-century composer is *The Nose* by the Russian Dmitry Shostakovich (1906–1975). It tells the story of Kovalyov, who loses his nose during a trip to the barber. The nose assumes a life of its own, and is eventually arrested by the police. When it is returned to its noseless owner, the nose at first refuses to stay on his face! The opera ends happily with the nose firmly attached once more to Kovalyov.

## MUSICALS

What is the difference between a musical and an opera? Musicals are usually much more light-hearted than operas, and often make use of thrilling dance routines. Also, there is often spoken dialogue in a musical, while operas usually have continuous music. The first hit musical was Jerome Kern's *Show Boat,* which took Broadway by storm in 1927. Other famous composers of musicals include Irving Berlin (1888–1989), Cole Porter (1891–1964), Richard Rogers (1902–1979), Leonard Bernstein (1918–1990), and Andrew Lloyd Webber (1948–).

## Expressionist opera

The expressionist movement began in the early 1900s. It used exaggeration and distortion to express violent emotion in both drama and art. Some composers used expressionism to create very dramatic operas, for example, the operas of the Austrian composers Arnold Schoenberg (1874–1945) and Alban Berg (1881–1951). The Hungarian Béla Bartók (1881–1945) wrote just one opera, *Bluebeard's Castle.* With its gruesome, nightmarish atmosphere, *Bluebeard's Castle* is typical of the expressionist style.

## Opera in the United States

A wide variety of opera has been created in the United States, ranging from *Porgy and Bess* by George Gershwin (1898–1937) to

*(left) George Gershwin*

*A Streetcar Named Desire* by André Previn (1929–). American composers frequently incorporate elements of jazz, blues, folk songs, and even electronic music in their compositions. Carlisle Floyd (1926–) is one of the most performed American composers and is noted for *Susannah, Of Mice and Men,* and *Cold Sassy Tree.*

*(left) Sidney Poitier in* Porgy and Bess

## Wind and waves

The British composer Benjamin Britten (1913–1976) lived in the Suffolk seaside town of Aldeburgh, England, and much of his music has associations with the sea. Britten's opera *Peter Grimes* is based on a poem by the Suffolk poet George Crabbe, and tells the story of a fisherman who is suspected of killing his apprentice. The opera was a huge success at its first performance in 1945 and encouraged other British composers to write operas, particularly Michael Tippett (1905–1998) and William Walton (1902–1983).

*(above) The beach at Aldeburgh, England, the seaside town in which Benjamin Britten lived*

## Opera and the news

The American composer John Adams (1947–) based two of his operas on real-life episodes from modern-day history. *Nixon in China*, completed in 1987, relates the events surrounding President Nixon's visit to China to meet Chairman Mao in 1972. *The Death of Klinghoffer*, written in 1991, tells the true story of the hijack of the cruise ship *Achille Lauro* in 1985, and the shooting of one of the hostages, the wheelchair-bound American Leon Klinghoffer.

### DID YOU KNOW?

Britten's opera *Billy Budd* is set at sea on the naval ship HMS *Indomitable*. The opera has no parts for women at all. Another of Britten's operas, *Owen Wingrave*, was written specially for television, although it has also been performed on the stage.

*(above) Benjamin Britten (1913–1976)*

## Opera for young people

Many composers have written operas to be performed and enjoyed by children. Britten's *The Little Sweep* and *Noye's Fludde* were both written for the annual music festival in Aldeburgh. *The Little Sweep* has a cast of adults and children, while *Noye's Fludde* was designed to be performed in a church and makes use of instruments such as recorders. Another British composer, Peter Maxwell Davies (1934–), has also written operas for children, such as *The Two Fiddlers* and *Cinderella*. At the Royal Opera House, Glyndebourne, and other opera houses, young people have worked with composers, designers, and directors to create their own operas. The production *Separation: The Story of Bullman and the Moonsisters*, staged in the Linbury Studio Theatre at the Royal Opera House in 1999, was performed entirely by children, who also wrote the words and music.

*(left) The 1999 production of* Separation: The Story of Bullman and the Moonsisters, *with its cast of children*

# Stories from the Opera

Many of the most famous operas are based on stories from mythology, history, or works of literature. These are adapted for the stage and set to music. Below are stories from some of the most popular operas. You can listen to extracts from them on the accompanying CD.

**DIE ZAUBERFLÖTE** (*The Magic Flute*)
*Music:* Wolfgang Amadeus Mozart
*Libretto:* Emanuel Schikaneder
*First performance:* Vienna, 1791
A fairy-tale opera about two lovers, Tamino and Pamina. It takes its name from the magic flute that protects Tamino from danger.

Tamino sees a picture of Pamina, daughter of the Queen of the Night, and falls madly in love with her. But she has been kidnapped by the high priest Sarastro. After many trials and tribulations, Tamino saves Pamina. They marry and live happily ever after.

*(above) Set design for the garden scene with the Sphinx in moonlight, from* The Magic Flute, *Act II, scene iii*

*(right) Act II from* The Magic Flute *by Mozart*

### DID YOU KNOW?

Despite the popularity of his music, Mozart remained poor because he preferred composing to playing in public. In those days, the rewards for composing an opera did not reflect the hard work involved. He was paid 450 gulden for *The Marriage of Figaro* – the sum of money he'd receive for playing just one concert!

*(right) A lively scene from Rossini's* The Barber of Seville

**BUSIEST MAN IN TOWN**

*The Barber of Seville*'s most famous aria is Figaro's "Largo al factotum" ("I Am the Busiest Man in Town"). Figaro sings that despite being a barber by trade, he is kept busy passing messages between secret lovers. He boasts about his cleverness. The music is busy and lively, just like Figaro's life, and it sets the comic mood of the opera.

**IL BARBIERE DI SIVIGLIA**
(*The Barber of Seville*)
*Music:* Gioacchino Rossini
*Libretto:* Cesare Sterbini
*First performance:* Rome, 1816
Dashing Count Almaviva is in love with beautiful Rosina, but her guardian, old Dr. Bartolo, wants to marry her himself. Figaro, the barber, helps the count meet Rosina. The count disguises himself as a drunken soldier and asks for lodgings in the doctor's house. When this fails, he returns disguised as Rosina's music teacher. When Bartolo discovers that the two lovers are planning to elope, he turns Rosina against the count. Just in time, Figaro saves the day, and the count and Rosina are married.

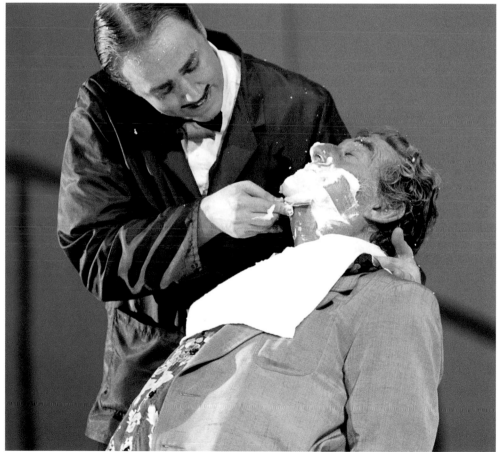

## L'ELISIR D'AMORE
*(The Elixir of Love)*
*Music:* Gaetano Donizetti
*Libretto:* Felice Romani
*First performance:* Milan, 1832
Bumbling farmer Nemorino is in love with Adina, who is pretty and rich. But so is handsome Sergeant Belcore. To capture Adina's heart, Nemorino buys what he thinks is a love potion from a visiting quack doctor. In fact, the potion turns out to be wine. Nemorino becomes drunk and makes a fool of himself. But Adina eventually agrees to marry him anyway. Then everyone wants some of the love potion!

## IL TROVATORE *(The Troubadour)*
*Music:* Giuseppe Verdi
*Libretto:* Salvatore Cammarano and Leone Emanuele Bardare
*First performance:* Rome, 1853
Set in Spain in the 1400s, this opera tells of Leonora, a noblewoman, and her lover, Manrico, a troubadour (poet-singer). But the Count Di Luna loves Leonora, too, and he imprisons Manrico. Only the gypsy woman Azucena knows that Manrico is actually the count's brother, who was kidnapped when an infant. She wants to take her revenge on the count because his father killed her mother. To save Manrico, Leonora promises to marry the count. She then drinks poison and dies. When the count has Manrico executed, Azucena announces that he has killed his own brother, and so has her revenge.

*(above) The doctor in* L'elisir d'amore, *with his so-called love potion*

*(right) Rigoletto, the court jester*

## RIGOLETTO

*Music:* Giuseppe Verdi
*Libretto:* Francesco Maria Piave
*First performance:* Venice, 1851
Based on a play by the famous French writer Victor Hugo, *Rigoletto* takes place at the court of the Italian Duke of Mantua. Rigoletto is the court jester. Through the courtiers' scheming, his daughter, Gilda, is kidnapped and taken to the duke. When Rigoletto finds her, he vows to take his revenge and pays an assassin to kill the duke. Tragically Gilda is stabbed instead.

## DIE WALKÜRE (*The Valkyrie*)

*Music:* Richard Wagner
*Libretto:* Richard Wagner
*First performance:* Munich, 1870
*Die Walküre* is the second opera in the great *Ring* cycle. Siegmund takes shelter in Hunding's hut, where he falls in love with Hunding's wife, Sieglinde. Jealous Hunding challenges him to a fight, but Sieglinde gives Siegmund a magic sword, and they are able to escape. Eventually, however, with the gods' help, Hunding kills Siegmund. The Valkyrie Brünnhilde, Siegmund's half-sister, picks up the pieces of his shattered sword and gives them to Sieglinde, who will soon give birth to Siegmund's child, the great hero Siegfried.

*(left) Giuseppe Verdi*

## DIE FLEDERMAUS (*The Bat*)

*Music:* Johann Strauss
*Libretto:* Carl Haffner and Richard Genée
*First performance:* Vienna, 1874

Three years earlier, Dr. Falke, disguised as a bat for a costume party, was made to walk home in broad daylight as a joke by his friend Eisenstein. Now in revenge, Dr. Falke invites Eisenstein to another costume party in order to expose his unfaithfulness. Eisenstein does not recognize his own wife, Rosalinde, or his maid, and he flirts with them shamelessly. Meanwhile, Rosalinde's admirer Alfred has been sent to prison in Eisenstein's place. Disguised as a lawyer, suspicious Eisenstein questions the pair about their friendship, but Rosalinde reminds him of the ball and he forgives them.

## CARMEN

*Music:* Georges Bizet
*Libretto:* Henri Meilhac and Ludovic Halévy
*First performance:* Paris, 1875

Set in Seville, Spain, *Carmen* is the tragic story of the doomed love affair between Carmen, a beautiful gypsy girl, and Don José, a soldier. When Carmen leaves Don José for the bullfighter Escamillo, Don José pleads for Carmen to return to him. Carmen refuses, and in a jealous rage, Don José stabs her to death.

(left) Denyce Graves as Carmen in 1994

**DID YOU KNOW?**

*Carmen*'s exciting plot and stirring music have made it one of the most popular operas of all. But its first performance was a failure. The Paris audience was upset by the lifestyle of the characters, which they thought was too immoral. Unfortunately, Bizet died three months after the premiere and did not enjoy the enormous popularity that *Carmen* soon achieved.

**DID YOU KNOW?**

The three most popular operas performed by The Royal Opera at the Royal Opera House since the company was founded in 1946 are *La bohème* (325 performances), *Aïda* (278), and *Carmen* (275).

*(above) Poster advertising a performance of* Tosca *in 1900*

*(right) Diana Soviero plays Cio-Cio-San in* Madama Butterfly

**A NIGHT AT THE OPERA**

Before watching an opera, find out as much as possible about it. Read the story and get to know a bit about the characters and how they behave. Listen to a recording of the music. This will make the experience even more enjoyable.

## TOSCA

*Music:* Giacomo Puccini
*Libretto:* Giuseppe Giacosa and Luigi Illica
*First performance:* Rome, 1900
The painter Cavaradossi hides escaped prisoner Angelotti in his villa. Cavaradossi's lover, Tosca, is tricked into telling the police, and Cavaradossi is sentenced to death. The police chief, Scarpia, agrees to release Cavaradossi if Tosca will be his mistress. Scarpia will pretend to have Cavaradossi shot but instead let the pair escape. But at the execution the bullets are real and Cavaradossi is killed. In despair, Tosca leaps to her death, having first killed Scarpia.

## MADAMA BUTTERFLY

*Music:* Giacomo Puccini
*Libretto:* Giuseppe Giacosa and Luigi Illica
*First performance:* Milan, 1904
The story of *Madama Butterfly* takes place in Japan around 1900. Cio-Cio-San (Madama Butterfly), a Japanese girl, falls in love with American naval officer B. F. Pinkerton. They marry, but Pinkerton leaves Japan with his ship. Cio-Cio-San gives birth to a son. Pinkerton returns to Japan with his new American wife. Heartbroken, Cio-Cio-San hands her son over to them, then commits suicide.

# Words and Music

How does an opera begin its life? Often a composer comes across a play, poem, or story that inspires him or her to jot down some musical ideas. But before these ideas can go much further, the composer needs a libretto – the words of the opera.

## Telling the story

Some composers are famous for writing their own librettos, like Richard Wagner and Michael Tippett. But most composers work with a person called a librettist, who prepares the words for an opera. The job of the librettist is to take the original story and adapt it so that it is suitable for opera. If the original idea comes from a novel, for example, the librettist will usually have to shorten and rewrite the text.

## What language?

In some opera houses, opera is always sung in the language in which it was written (so Verdi's operas are only heard in Italian and Wagner's in German). Other opera houses allow operas to be sung in translation (so an English or American audience may hear the words in English). There is another solution, though. Many opera houses now have supertitles (surtitles) – a translation of the words being sung displayed on a screen just above the stage.

### DID YOU KNOW?

As an alternative to the screen above the stage, the Metropolitan Opera House in New York City and the Santa Fe Opera, USA, have a small screen mounted in front of every seat. The translation of the words is displayed on this screen, and it can be switched on or off by the viewer.

*(left) Use of supertitles (surtitles) during a Royal Opera House performance of* La traviata *broadcast outdoors, in Covent Garden, London*

Arthur Sullivan and William S. Gilbert are one of the most famous partnerships in operatic history. They wrote comic-style operas known as operettas. These have all the elements of an opera but include some spoken dialogue. *Trial by Jury*, written in 1875, did so well that the impresario Richard D'Oyly Carte set up a theatre company exclusively to perform their works.

*(below) D'Oyly Carte, the theatre company set up to perform the works of Gilbert and Sullivan*

## Famous partnerships

The librettist plays a very important part in the creation of an opera. Yet it is the composer's name that is usually associated with the finished opera, and the librettist often gets forgotten! Nevertheless, there have been famous partnerships between librettists and composers in the history of opera:

### Wolfgang Amadeus Mozart and Lorenzo Da Ponte

Da Ponte was poet at the court of Emperor Joseph II in Vienna. He persuaded the emperor to allow Mozart to write *The Marriage of Figaro,* which was based on a scandalous play that had already been banned in France. He also wrote the librettos for *Don Giovanni* and *Così fan tutte.*

### Richard Strauss and Hugo von Hofmannsthal

Hofmannsthal wrote the librettos for six of Strauss's operas, including *Der Rosenkavalier* and *Elektra*. Strauss was so impressed with Hofmannsthal's work that he once wrote to him: "We were born for one another and are certain to do fine things together if you remain faithful to me."

### Arthur Sullivan and William S. Gilbert

Sullivan wrote the music and Gilbert wrote the words in this famous partnership. The result was a stream of comic operettas, including *HMS Pinafore, The Pirates of Penzance,* and *The Mikado.*

## Voices for opera

There are four main types of singing voice: the high female voice is called soprano; the lower female voice is contralto; the high male voice is tenor; and the low male voice is bass. In opera, there are in-between voices, too. Here are just a few of these operatic variations:

**coloratura soprano:** a very high female voice, often performing elaborate music with lots of trills, scales, and thrilling high notes

**mezzo-soprano:** lies between the soprano and contralto voice

**countertenor:** the highest male voice, can sing in the same range as the female contraltos by training the voice to sing falsetto (high)

**heldentenor** (heroic tenor): a strong, dramatic tenor used in German opera

**baritone:** lies between the bass and the tenor

**basso profundo:** a very deep male voice, lower than a normal bass

### CROWD SCENES

Most operas include a part for a chorus, usually made up of the four main types of singing voice. The chorus adds activity and interest, and gives the composer the chance to contrast the sounds of lots of singing voices against the solo sound of the principals.

*(left) A curtain call for* Die Meistersinger von Nürnberg, *showing principals and chorus, with the chorus director in the middle, applauding the cast*

*(above) The baritone Thomas Allen as Don Giovanni in 1992*

## Principal sounds

The singers who perform the leading roles in an opera are called the principals. Often the heroine and hero parts are sung by a soprano and a tenor. For example, in Puccini's *La bohème* the heroine Mimì is a soprano and the hero Rodolfo is a tenor. Of course, there are many famous exceptions: Carmen is a mezzo-soprano, and Don Giovanni is a baritone.

## In the pit

s the audience sits enthralled by the action onstage, it's easy to forget there is a whole orchestra playing, too. The orchestra sits in the orchestra pit, in front of and beneath the stage, partly hidden from the audience. The conductor is the vital link between orchestra and performers. He or she gives the singers their cues – indicating when they should start singing. The conductor must also control the volume, ensuring that the orchestra does not overpower the singers!

### DID YOU KNOW?

In seventeenth-century Italy it was considered scandalous for a woman to appear onstage, so women's roles in opera were usually sung by men. These men were known as *castrati*, and they were the superstars of the opera world. One of the most famous was Carlo Farinelli (1705–1782), who was renowed for the purity and agility of his voice.

*(left) The orchestra pit*

# Putting on an Opera

It's the first night of a new production of an opera. The audience settles into its seats, the orchestra plays the overture, and the curtain goes up. What the audience is seeing and hearing is the result of months, if not years, of careful planning and hard work. So what does it take to put on an opera?

## Working as a team

The conductor and his or her team are in charge of the musical quality of the opera, making sure everyone knows the musical score. The theatrical side of the opera is the responsibility of the director, who organizes and guides everything that happens onstage. The director's ideas for the production are interpreted by the designer, who is in charge of the sets, costumes, and props. For a good production, it is vital that these three people work closely together.

*(below) A set from* The Magic Flute

## Designing the set

It is up to the director and the designer to decide on the look and feel of a production. Will the set be very elaborate or very simple? Will it be modern or a period opera? Scale models are made of every set to be used in the production. Once these are approved, the models are used by the set builders to create full-size versions.

(left) Designer Zandra Rhodes adjusts the costume of Papagena. This is the first time the singer, New Zealand soprano Annelies Chapman, has seen the costume for her character.

(above) Zandra Rhodes's original sketch for Papagena, the bird-girl, in a new production of Mozart's The Magic Flute for the San Diego Opera. This is fashion designer Zandra Rhodes's first venture into designing costumes for opera.

## Costume design

C ostume designs for an opera are often decided up to a year before the opening night. The designer meets with members of the costume department to discuss the period and style of the opera. They work together to choose fabrics, then prepare a model of each costume using a cotton material for final approval. Then they cut the chosen fabric and start work on the actual costume. Costumes must be designed so that they are not too tight around the throat and chest, so the singers can breathe easily.

## The wig department

**W**igs are a very important part of the opera costume. The wig department at the Royal Opera House in London has ten staff members who make between 200 and 2,000 wigs every year. All the wigs are made by hand from human hair and require a great deal of time to create – the strands of hair must be sewn in one by one! Every wig is made in three different sizes so there will always be one that fits a particular singer if the production is put on again in future years. At the end of the production, the wig is cleaned and stored. (The Royal Opera House has up to 40,000 wigs in storage.)

*(right) Wigs form a crucial part of any opera costume*

**DID YOU KNOW?**

While singing the role of Tosca, the opera star Maria Callas once leaned too close to a candle flame during a performance, and her wig caught fire. Tito Gobbi, playing the villainous Scarpia, quickly leaned over and put out the fire with his bare hands. Maria Callas didn't miss a note!

*(below) Mezzo-soprano Adria Firestone is transformed for her role as the witch Rosina Daintymouth in Engelbert Humperdinck's Hansel and Gretel*

**DID YOU KNOW?**

At the Royal Opera House, the fly tower above the stage, where the lights and scenery are suspended, is 37m (121 feet) high.

**GET SET, GO!**

In most opera houses around the world, there are several productions being rehearsed and performed at the same time. It is essential that sets can be moved around quickly backstage. At the Royal Opera House, sets are moved round on computer-operated wagons. This system means three different productions can be set up onstage and taken down in the course of one day.

## Props

Tables, chairs, cups and saucers, tankards, spears, flowers, books – all these items, and often more, might be needed in an opera production, and they are all the responsibility of the props department. The word *prop* is an abbreviation of "property of the stage," and it refers to anything that is additional to the fixed scenery. Some productions call for very unusual props. For example, in Richard Wagner's *Parsifal*, a dead swan falls out of the sky.

*(left) A decorative frontcloth for a production of* The Magic Flute

*(below) An intricate set construction for* Madama Butterfly

## Rehearsing an opera

The earliest musical rehearsals are held not onstage but in studios, often away from the opera house. It can take several weeks for everyone to learn the music thoroughly, and to create the stage movement as determined by the director. The principals, chorus, and orchestra rehearse separately at first, then come together in a *sitzprobe* (German for "seated rehearsal"). Then rehearsals begin on the set for the opera. It is important that the singers have time to get used to the design of the set, as well as the costumes and props. The dress rehearsal is the last one before the production opens to the public.

# Famous Opera Houses

Opera houses are often very lavish and impressive places, designed for people to have a special night out. But you don't need a grand opera house to put on an opera. Small-scale operas are produced in the most unexpected places, from barns to church halls.

## Wagner's opera house

R ichard Wagner dreamed of building an opera house specifically designed for his own operas. His dream came true when the town of Bayreuth in Germany gave him a plot of land and King Ludwig II of Bavaria provided a large donation. Wagner wanted people to watch his operas without any distractions, so the auditorium was built from wood with none of the plush decorations of the day. He insisted that the auditorium lights be darkened for performances, and almost completely hid the orchestra pit from the view of the audience by sinking it deep underneath the stage. The first performance to be given in Wagner's Festspielhaus in Bayreuth was the *Ring* cycle in 1876 (see pages 20–21).

*(below) The Richard Wagner Theatre in Bavaria, Germany*

*(left) The auditorium of the Royal Opera House*

*(above) A view of the Floral Hall and façade of the newly renovated Royal Opera House, Covent Garden, in London*

## DID YOU KNOW?

In the early eighteenth century in London and Paris, the really expensive seats at the opera were actually on the stage. Wealthy members of the audience liked to get as close as possible to the famous opera stars!

For many families in the nineteenth century, an opera box was like a second home, decorated to their own taste. In some opera houses, if they got bored with the action onstage, they could even draw the curtains to cut themselves off from the auditorium and have a quick game of cards!

## Rebuilding the Royal Opera House

The first building on the site of the Royal Opera House, Covent Garden, in London, England, was built as early as 1732, but it burned down in 1808. Its replacement was also destroyed by fire only forty-eight years later. The present opera house dates from 1858, but by the 1990s it needed major improvements. So in 1997, the opera house shut down and the building work began. When it reopened in 1999, the public areas and the area backstage were transformed.

## Horseshoe houses

Most opera houses built before the end of the nineteenth century were modeled on the style of opera houses in Italy. The auditorium was a horseshoe shape, with the stage at the open end. The floor of the auditorium, known as the stalls, was filled with benches – the cheap seats – while the wealthier people sat in boxes that were arranged in up to six tiers overlooking the stage.

*(right) The main façade of La Scala, Milan, Italy*

## Top houses

**T**here are many celebrated opera houses around the world. Here are just a few:

**La Scala, Milan, Italy:** Built in 1778, although it was rebuilt after bomb damage during World War II; one of the grandest houses in the world.

**Teatro Colón, Buenos Aires, Argentina:** Built in 1908, this huge theatre holds up to 4,000 audience members.

**Opéra Bastille, Paris, France:** Built in 1990, the auditorium is ultra-modern, with two balconies above the stalls.

**Drottningholm Court Theatre, Swedish Royal Palace, Sweden:** Built in 1766, this tiny theatre holds only 500 people; backstage, much of the original machinery is still working.

**Royal Opera House, London, England:** Present opera house dates from 1858, but modernized in 1999 (page 43).

**Metropolitan Opera, Lincoln Center, New York, USA:** Built in 1966 and home to the Metropolitan Opera Company, it attracts opera stars from all over the world.

### BEIJING OPERA

In China, opera has been performed for many centuries. Chinese operas are often based on folklore and history. In the past, operas performed at the Emperor's court were often very formal, and very long – lasting five or six hours. Chinese folk opera is much more informal and often includes acrobatics, mime, and dancing.

*(below) The Metropolitan Opera House, Lincoln Center, New York*

## The Sydney Opera House

One of the most famous landmarks in the world, the Sydney Opera House stands on Bennelong Point in Sydney Harbour. Its famous shell-shaped roofs were designed by Danish architect Jorn Utzon. At first no one could agree on how these complex roofs could be built. After years of argument, Utzon resigned from the project and, amazingly, he has never visited the completed building. The opera house opened in 1973.

## Opera festivals

Probably the most famous opera festival in Europe is held in Mozart's birthplace: Salzburg, Austria. The small town of Wexford in Ireland is host to an opera festival every autumn for rarely performed operas. Every summer there is a season of opera performances at Glyndebourne, a beautiful country house with an opera house attached in Sussex, England. During the long interval in the middle of the Glyndebourne operas, the audience picnics in the gardens. A similar type of festival is held at Glimmerglass, near New York City, USA.

*(left) Picnicking at Glyndebourne*

# Singing Stars

Many singers do not start to train for opera until their voices are mature enough to withstand the demands of opera roles. Even then, a beautiful voice is not enough if you want to become an operatic star. You also need acting ability, a good memory, and nerves of steel!

**DID YOU KNOW?**

One of the earliest female opera stars was Anna Renzi (1620–1660). She was the first person to sing the role of Emperor Nero's wife in Claudio Monteverdi's opera *L'incoronazione di Poppea* (*The Coronation of Poppaea*, see page 12). She was renowned throughout Venice not only for her beautiful voice but also for her acting skills.

## Voice projection

When an opera singer opens his or her mouth and sings, the sound must travel right to the back of a large theatre. Unlike pop stars, opera singers cannot rely on microphones to amplify their voices – this has to be done naturally. But it isn't just a case of singing loudly. The singer has to "project" the voice, so that even the quietest melody can be heard clearly at the back of the auditorium. This takes years of careful training.

## The importance of breathing

When you sing or speak, breath passes over your vocal cords, making them vibrate. Of course, we all breathe in and out without even thinking about it, but controlling the breath is one of the most important things opera singers must learn. They do this by using the diaphragm, the large muscle that lies beneath the lungs. The diaphragm helps to control the flow of breath out of the lungs so the air doesn't rush out all at once. With good breath control a singer can sing a long phrase of music and make it sound effortless.

(below) Opera singers have to rely on the natural projection of the voice – they don't use microphones

## Difficult divas

(above) The famous soprano Joan Sutherland preparing for a performance. Opera singers must take great care of their voices and their health in order to match the demands of opera performances.

### NELLIE MELBA

The Australian opera singer Nellie Melba (1861–1931) became so famous that she gave her name to a type of pudding (Peach Melba). Her coloratura soprano voice was admired the world over, but she also had a reputation for being a terrible prima donna. Once, at the end of a performance in London, the tenor principal made the mistake of stepping onstage to take a bow with her. She pushed him back viciously, saying: "In this house, nobody takes a bow with Nellie Melba!"

Some opera stars have reputations for being difficult and demanding. But life as an opera singer is hard work. Singers' voices and bodies must be kept in top condition at all times. They have to get plenty of sleep, avoid eating foods that affect the voice, and, most of all, avoid getting sick. Catching a cold is every singer's nightmare. So it is little wonder that many singers seem obsessive about such things as avoiding chills, or rooms that are too hot … or too cold … or too damp … or too dry!

(left) Nellie Melba – a difficult diva?

## Enrico Caruso

E nrico Caruso (1873–1921) is said to have had one of the most beautiful tenor voices the world has ever known. He was one of twenty children born in Naples, Italy, to a poor family. He received little education, musical or otherwise. Yet with his natural talents he shot to international fame in the late 1890s. In 1903 he made his debut at the Metropolitan Opera House ("the Met") in New York City. American audiences loved him, and he appeared at the Met hundreds of times before the end of his career, in 1920. You can hear Caruso's voice for yourself because he made many recordings.

*(left) The tenor Enrico Caruso (1873–1921)*

### STARS OF TODAY

**Jessye Norman** (1945–) American soprano, with a huge, rich voice and a commanding stage presence. Although her appearances onstage are quite rare today, she has made many notable recordings.

**Barbara Bonney** (1956–) American soprano, with a beautiful, high, clear voice. She made her debut with Vienna State Opera in 1984 as Sophie in *Der Rosenkavalier*.

**Kiri Te Kanawa** (1944–) New Zealand soprano known for her interpretations of roles by Mozart and Strauss.

**Bryn Terfel** (1965–) Welsh bass-baritone. He won the Lieder Prize in the 1989 Cardiff Singer of the World Competition and has since shot to fame.

**Cecilia Bartoli** (1966–) Italian mezzo-soprano. Daughter of two opera singers, she has a spectacular, agile, warm voice with a wide range.

**The Three Tenors** (see page 49).

(left) The Three Tenors – the best-known stars of modern opera

## Maria Callas

(left) Maria Callas as Violetta in La traviata

The American-Greek soprano Maria Callas (1923–1977) was born in New York City, but both her parents were Greek. She returned to Greece when she was thirteen years old and made her operatic debut at age fifteen, in Athens in *Cavalleria rusticana* (*Rustic Chivalry*) by Pietro Mascagni (1863–1945). During her career, she was able to sing a wide variety of roles because she could reach the top notes of a coloratura soprano as well as the powerful lower notes of a mezzo-soprano.

# About the CD

**1 *Die Fledermaus (The Bat):* Overture**
Johann Strauss's light-hearted operetta *The Bat* pokes fun at lying wives, deceiving husbands, cheating servants, and rich, bored aristocrats. The subject matter may be uncomfortable, but the tone is always frothy, and is perfectly established right from the first note of this toe-tapping overture. Strauss was famous for his waltzes (such as "The Blue Danube"), and includes a wonderful one in this opera.

**2 *Rigoletto:* "La donna è mobile"**
The dashing but heartless Duke of Mantua has come to a lonely tavern for a rendezvous. While waiting, he amuses himself by singing this jolly song, which is all about the unfaithfulness of women. He doesn't realize, however, that his faithful, broken-hearted lover, Gilda, and her angry father, Rigoletto, are outside listening to him.

**3 *Madama Butterfly:* "Humming Chorus"**
Madama Butterfly is a young Japanese woman who has not seen her American husband for three years. When she believes he is about to return, she decorates her little house with beautiful flowers and prepares to wait for his arrival. The magical stillness of the "Humming Chorus" is heard in the distance, and musically paints Butterfly's long night of waiting and tragic optimism.

**4 *Il barbiere di Siviglia (The Barber of Seville):* "Largo al factotum"**
Figaro is one of the local barbers of Seville, but in this famous tongue-twisting aria (which he sings when he first appears onstage), he reveals that he actually does a lot more than cut hair and shave chins: he is a surgeon and a romantic go-between, too. The scampering, flighty music suggests how busy he is, but also that he is full of energy and fun.

**5 *Il barbiere di Siviglia (The Barber of Seville):* "Temporale"**
When feisty Rosina believes that her lover has betrayed her, she angrily agrees to marry her cunning old guardian. A storm then breaks outside, and the weather perfectly mirrors her state of mind. It begins with little drops of rain and tiny splashes of water and builds into a thunderous downpour, but the composer keeps the overall effect light and comical – and thus hints that there will be a happy ending for Rosina and her lover.

**6 *Die Walküre (The Valkyrie):* "Ride of the Valkyries"**
The nine Valkyries are warrior-maidens who ride through the sky on powerful horses. Their job is to fly into battles, collect the bodies of heroes who have been killed, and take them to Valhalla, the

home of the gods. In the breathtaking "Ride of the Valkyries," Wagner shows them at work. The music reflects their fierce energy, their thrill at being in battle, and the thundering of their horses' hooves.

### 7 *Tosca:* "Io de' sospiri"

Cavaradossi is a painter who has been sentenced to death for political reasons. In the cold hour before dawn, as he sits in his cell waiting for his execution, he hears the bells of a flock of sheep and the voice of a young shepherd boy in the distance. The boy (one of the few roles for children in opera) sings a sad little ballad of scorned love.

### 8 *Il trovatore (The Troubadour):* "Anvil Chorus"

Like the previous piece, this one is set at dawn, although the moods in each couldn't be more different. Here a group of industrious gypsies are beginning their working day, and to encourage themselves, they sing a jolly song about pretty gypsy girls. In a masterstroke of orchestration, the composer has added the banging of their anvils as accompaniment to the song.

### 9 *Die Zauberflöte (The Magic Flute):* "Der Hölle Rache kocht in meinem Herzen"

In the first act of *The Magic Flute*, the Queen of the Night seems to be a good character who is anxious about her kidnapped daughter, Pamina. In this aria from the second act, she reveals that she is actually quite wicked – she orders Pamina to murder the high priest Sarastro. The music is incredibly high and difficult, and it wonderfully portrays the queen's flashing temper and haughty manner.

### 10 *Carmen:* "Habanera"

Carmen is a passionate, unpredictable Spanish gypsy who works in a cigarette factory. When she enters the town square during a short break from work, she sings this seductive, electrifying melody to a group of local people and to a young soldier who appears to be ignoring her. (It is Don José, the hero of the opera.) The song suggests that love is fickle and that it grows and dies quickly.

### 11 *L'elisir d'amore (The Elixir of Love):* "Udite udite, o rustici"

Dr. Dulcamara is nothing more than a quack, and the "miraculous" potion that he sells is simply wine. When he arrives in one small Italian village, he sings the townsfolk this wonderfully comic aria full of outrageous claims for his product. He asserts, for example, that it will cure a broken heart, get rid of warts, and (most important for the plot) act as a love potion. Needless to say, the villagers believe every word.

# Index

# Glossary

**aria** A sung solo that expresses a character's feelings.

**baritone** A male voice that lies between the bass and tenor range.

**bass** A low male voice.

**basso profundo** A very deep male voice, lower than a normal bass.

**bel canto** Meaning "beautiful singing" in Italian, this style of singing emphasizes the quality of tone, range, and an ability to sing high notes without strain.

**castrati** A male singer who took the part of a woman in seventeenth-century Italian operas. Castrati were greatly admired for their melodious and very high singing voices.

**classical** The classical movement in music lasted from around 1750 to 1820. In opera, it describes a style that was graceful, with believable plots and stirring music.

**coloratura soprano** A very high female voice, often required to sing elaborate music with trills, scales, and incredibly high notes.

**countertenor** The highest male voice (also known as alto). Can sing same range as female contralto by training voice to sing falsetto.

**expressionism** The name originally given to an art movement in the early 1900s. In art and drama it is used to express violent emotion through exaggeration and distortion. Some composers used expressionism to create very dramatic, atmospheric operas.

**falsetto** A male voice used to reach a higher pitch than usual. Also, a style of singing used by tenors for notes that lie above the normal range, sometimes for comic effect.

**folk opera** American style of opera, using folk styles of music such as jazz and blues. The best-known example is Gershwin's *Porgy and Bess*.

**grand opera** Popular in the nineteenth century, these operas were spectacular events with dramatic music, exotic stage sets, and usually a huge cast of singers, and even animals onstage.

**heldentenor** Meaning literally "heroic tenor," this strong dramatic male voice is used in German opera.

**leitmotif** A short passage of music that identifies a particular character, place, or idea. These pieces, or themes, are repeated as reminders throughout the opera. This device was used frequently by Wagner, particularly in his *Ring* cycle.

**libretto** The words or story of an opera, written by a librettist.

**mezzo-soprano** Female singing voice that lies between the soprano and contralto in range.

**modern opera** Operas created in the twentieth century. They have "experimental" plots such as nonsense stories, and different types of musical sounds and styles, like jazz, or cabaret music.

**nationalist opera** A style developed by composers at the beginning of the twentieth century to express pride in the music of their country. These operas were often based on traditional folk stories, and included national folk tunes and folk instruments.

**opera buffa** Meaning "comic opera" in Italian, these began as short comic acts performed during a long opera seria. Later they became complete operas, based on more everyday, comic events.

**opera seria** Meaning "serious opera" in Italian, this type of opera was popular in the seventeenth century. Usually based on Greek or Roman legends, they were dramatic, often complicated, and long.

**operetta** Comic-style opera using a more popular style of music, also called "light opera." The most famous operettas are by Gilbert and Sullivan.

**orchestra pit** The space in front of and below the stage, where the orchestra usually plays during an opera.

**overture** A piece of orchestral music played at the beginning of an opera or ballet.

**principal** A leading role in an opera.

**prop** An item required onstage to assist singers or actors, e.g., furniture, books, cups, saucers, glasses, spears, etc.

**recitative** The part of the text that tells the audience about the plot and moves the action on. It is sung in a speechlike way.

**Romantic** A musical movement popular in the nineteenth century. Romantic operas told the stories of nature or folklore, and were expressive and emotional.

**score** The written music showing how all the vocal and instrumental parts should be sung and played. The composer works closely with a librettist when writing an opera score.

**set** The scenery and overall stage design, created by a set designer, who works closely with the opera director and designer. An opera house must be able to store and move many sets for different productions at any one time.

***sitzprobe*** A seated rehearsal.

**soprano** The high female voice.

**supertitles (surtitles)** A translation of the words of the opera, displayed as they are being sung, on a screen above the stage.

**tenor** The high male voice.

***verismo* opera** Realistic and dramatic style of early twentieth-century opera, which used real-life stories based on contemporary events.

# Acknowledgments

Many thanks to the Royal Opera House, especially Paul Reeve (Education) and Francesca Franchi (Archives) for acting as consultants for this book, and to Jane Jackson (Archives). Many of the photographs used are from the archives of the Royal Opera House, which were kindly made available to us. Thanks also to Ian Campbell of the San Diego Opera for his help in providing assistance and information, particularly on American opera. Thanks to Jo Fletcher-Watson for her project-editing work, to Felicity Harvey for the picture research, and to Nigel Partridge for designing the book.

The publisher would like to thank all those who supplied photographs for this book. The copyright owners are listed below:
Catherine Ashmore: front cover image, back cover (main image), 18 (bottom right), 21 (middle left), 22, 24, 32, 33 (bottom), 37 (top left), 41 (bottom left), 56
Clive Barda/Performing Arts Library: back cover (inset), 6, 19, 21 (bottom right), 23 (bottom right), 30, 36, 40 (left)
Bettmann/CORBIS: 25 (bottom left), 44 (bottom), 47 (bottom)
Bill Cooper: 29 (bottom right), 34, 38, 41 (top right), 43 (top right) (with Image Hayes Davidson), 46 (bottom right)
Dominic Photography: 8, 31
Fotomas Index UK: 10
Courtesy of Glyndebourne Festival Opera/CORBIS: 45
ML Hart: 2, 9, 39 (left), 39 (right), 40 (middle right)
Hulton-Deutsch Collection/Corbis: 25 (right)
Peter Mackertitch, Paris: 43 (top left)
Ira Nowinski/CORBIS: 47 (top left)
Reuters New Media Inc./CORBIS: 49 (top)
Royal Opera House Archive Office: 16 (engraving by E Finden 1833), 20, 23 (bottom left), 27 (middle left) (© Clive Strutt), 31, 48
Marcus Tate: 27 (bottom)
V&A Picture Library: 49 (bottom left)
Reg Wilson: 13 (bottom)

Bridgeman Art Library: 11 [bottom] (Julian Hartnoll, UK), 12 [bottom], 12–13 [top], 14, 15 [top] (City of Westminster Archive Centre), 15 [bottom right], 17 [bottom right] (Roger-Viollet, Paris), 17 [top left] (Haags Gemeentemuseum, Netherlands), 18 [bottom left], 20 [middle] (Roger-Viollet, Paris), 26 [top] (Victoria & Albert Museum, London), 28 [bottom] (Historisches Museum der Stadt, Vienna), 28–29 [middle] (Deutsches Theatermuseum, Munich), 33 [top left], 35 [bottom left], 37 [bottom] (© Fermin Rocker, c/o Bartley Drey Gallery, London), 42 [bottom right] (Roger-Viollet, Paris), 44 [top left]

Every effort has been made to trace the copyright holder for each photograph, but on occasion this has not been possible. The publisher is happy to correct any omission in future printings.

*Endpiece: A scene from a Royal Opera production of* The Bartered Bride *in 1998*